By Newton F. Tolman

NORTH OF MONADNOCK
OUR LOONS ARE ALWAYS LAUGHING
IN SEARCH OF GENERAL MILES
HISTORY OF WESTMINSTER, MASS.
HISTORY OF ACWORTH, N. H.
NELSON MUSIC COLLECTION (WITH KAY GILBERT)
QUICK TUNES AND GOOD TIMES

QUICK TUNES

AND

GOOD TIMES

A LIGHT-HEARTED GUIDE TO
JIGS, REELS, RANTS, PLANXTYS, AND
OTHER LITTLE-KNOWN NEW ENGLAND
FOLK MUSIC

BY NEWTON F. TOLMAN

WILLIAM L. BAUHAN • PUBLISHER

DUBLIN • NEW HAMPSHIRE

A few parts of this book have been seen, in one form or another, by readers of the *Berkshire Eagle, Yankee,* and *The Nelson Music Collection.*

CONTENTS

LARGO'S FAIRY DANCE

Composed (by the desire) & Dedicated to the Members of the

Fife Hunt

By

NATH: GOW.

To which is added **LORD RAMSAY'S** Strathspey
and a Favorite New Valtz.

Price ——————————————————— 1/

*Edin? Printed and Sold by Gow & Shepherd N? 16 Princes Street and to be had of John Gow N? 31.
Carnaby Street Golden Square London.*

The Fairies Advancing — a Slow March.

by Nath: Gow.

Dolce Piano

The Fairy Dance.

by Nath: Gow

with spirit

(5)

From Nathaniel Gow's *Complete Repository*, published
in Edinburgh about 1800. See Chapter Seven.

Author's Note

In the past few years, so many people have stopped by to ask about our music, and we have spent so much time trying to explain it, the natural solution was to put the whole story into a book of some sort. I had done a few articles on the current square dance scene for the *Berkshire Eagle,* but they contained little about the music itself and its history .

Many more such inquiries followed the publication, in 1969, of *The Nelson Music Collection,* compiled by Kay Gilbert and myself. Begun as a notebook for our own use, this developed into the first modern printing of a highly selective collection of authentic scores of square dance melodies.

The ever increasing interest in folk music of all sorts pointed up one fact I hadn't thought about very much in the past. It seemed that the average music lovers, and the musicians themselves, of the present day, might know something about the traditional music of Andalusia, or India, or Ghana; but about our own old New

England square dance music, nothing at all.

An incident of the other day was typical. Some friends dropped in for a cup of tea or whatever, bringing with them a young composer who was staying at the nearby MacDowell Colony.

Noticing some sheets of music lying around the typewriter on my desk, the composer said, "Do you mind if I ask what you're working on?"

"Not at all," I answered. "I've just been running through a hundred or so hornpipes, trying to pick out some examples to include in a book. . . ."

"Just what *is* a hornpipe?" he asked.

Here was a chap who had taken top honors at one of the best music schools, done graduate work abroad, and written some things which had won him high praise. Yet he didn't know a hornpipe from a reel or a jig or a strathspey, and he had never heard any authentic old square dance music in all his life. It should be added that after he had heard us play a couple of our old melodies, he was delighted, and didn't want us to stop.

And so it is the main purpose of the following chapters, together with a few scores included, to explain the basic nature of this music.

As for the great numbers of people who now casually enjoy square dancing here or there, if they ever had a chance to dance to really good square dance music, they would find themselves lifted right off their feet. But that is a side-issue here. The aim of this book is to make a convincing case for square dance music as something that can be *listened to* with pleasure. Something well worth playing for its own sake by expert musicians, and not merely by duffers. And above all, the distinction must be made between this music and the stuff that has so generally been heard.

If this is also something of a musical autobiography, it is only because most of us find any discourse on music alone, with the people left out, dull reading at best. And please don't forget — musicians, of whatever kind, are apt to be opinionated and sometimes cantankerous in their views. But I've tried to follow a precept of Hemingway's: tell it like it is.

NEWTON F. TOLMAN

In the early 1900's square dance bands dressed for the occasion — and the photographer. A typical New England band of the period.

Before Folks Talked About "Folk Music"

IT SEEMS ODD NOW, looking back some fifty years, how little I liked having to play any kind of square dance music when I was a boy. It was almost as bad as some of my other chores, like milking cows. Even practicing scales and exercises from Duverge's *Method For The Boehm Flute* was more fun.

I envied the early jazz musicians, and sometimes wished my family had bought me a saxophone instead of a flute. In those days the flute was almost the forgotten instrument, even in symphonic music. My flute embarrassed me. People were always asking, "Say, what is that thing you're playing on, anyway?"

My father must have started me on a fife when I was very small; I can't even remember just when I was first parading with the village fife-and-drum corps. The old Civil War veteran who had been the only fifer had died, and I was evidently considered better than nothing to replace him, on such important occasions as Decoration Day and the Fourth of July.

By age eight or so I had got hold of an old wooden flute. Its six finger holes were augmented by a few metal keys, making a chromatic scale more or less possible.

A couple of years later my father's Cousin Percy, a very talented musician — and like all flautists, a trifle eccentric — persuaded my parents to mortgage the farm and buy me a first-class Haynes silver flute he had selected. Cousin Percy and his rich but miserly wife had a cottage at the farm. Every summer he gave me daily lessons; a good teacher, but tougher and more demanding than a Marine drill sergeant. "Don't slur! Articulate! *Tu-ku, tu-ku, tu-ku, tu-ku, tu-ku, tu-ku.* Now play that arpeggio one hundred times — and if you can't hit all the notes after that, damn it, play it another hundred times!" No tunes, ever. Just scales and exercises.

All during my growing-up years, like it or not, I had to play square dance music a good deal. It was the music my father knew best, and my brother and I had to help "entertain the summer folks" with our family concerts several times a week. Father on drums or cornet, my brother on piano, and often some other old-timers sitting in with us.

We also had to compete with thunderstorms. One of our "star boarders" for several years was a Boston matron who was deathly afraid of thunder and lightning. At the first distant rumble of thunder, at any hour during the day or night, my mother would hurry us all into the living room with our instruments. We would have to start whanging away, as loud as we could play, and keep it up as long as the storm lasted. Poor Mrs. Porter would be lying on the couch, covered with blankets and shawls and pillows, moaning and screeching, while we tried our best to drown out every thunderclap with any improvised crescendo we could think of.

The old music we played had very little in common with all the stuff that has become generally known as square dance music during the past thirty years or so. This fact will be examined in more technical detail in further chapters — as painlessly as possible, I hope.

Even in those early days, my brother and I had made a start toward acquiring some sense of discrimination. My brother had a flair for showmanship, and was always aware of what our listeners liked best to hear us play. Though these summer people came from far and wide, and they had no idea what the term "square dance music" meant, many of them responded to it with very genuine enthusiasm whenever we played it.

Our old music had been handed down in the family from generations back. Square dancing itself was no longer done when I was small, except maybe once or twice in the winter, when the older folks would gather in the town hall for a "sociable." (Always pronounced "social.") Survivors of the old Nelson town orchestra would assemble, and play the music that had still been in vogue when they were young, and there would be dancing after supper. The last of these ensembles ever to play in the town hall (most had died not long afterward, by the time I was twelve or so) included, as nearly as I can recall, nine musicians. We had a piano, bass viol, cornet, two first violins, two second violins, clarinet, and flute. We used the old orchestrations, and each of us had his own part to read for each number we played.

Old Wallace Dunn, auctioneer and town Moderator, was the prompter for the dancing. (The term "caller" and the practice of singing the calls, came years later when square dancing was popularly revived. About 1930, in our region.) The sound of the music that evening fifty years ago, though I have never heard anything like it since, still comes to mind sometimes when we again play some of the same old melodies.

Another part of my earlier musical experience came from playing with country bands. They had nothing to do with the square dance music scene, but I can't resist making a brief mention of them, while on the subject of musical nostalgia.

Our own town of Nelson, New Hampshire had grown too small to support a band of its own since my father's young days, but I played sometimes with bands from neighboring towns. Almost every village and town common then had its raised bandstand — most of them now removed by forward-looking "planners" to make way for filling stations or parking lots.

At the annual Nelson Old Home Day celebration down in the old picnic grove, the Harrisville band would play for an hour after lunch. Then they would mostly sit around on the back of the bandstand while the speaking droned on, and afterward play again to end the program.

On one such occasion, when the interminable speeches seemed to be nearing an end (there were then about a dozen elderly or vacationing ministers among the summer residents) the chairman announced that the band would close the program — unless someone else would still like to be heard from.

At this point old George Higgins, the alto horn player, drunker than usual, jumped up and staggered forward. (My father always said one of my uncles, who had a reputation as the principal village practical joker, had put him up to it.) Pausing dramatically at the front of the platform, George shouted at the top of his lungs, "My friends, I would just like to ask, where was Andrew Jackson in those perilous times? Where? . . . . Why, up to his ass in blood and guts and thunder!"

In the awed silence that followed this brief oration, old George turned around and jumped over the back railing and disappeared into the thick woods below.

Years later, after he died, I bought George's ancient brass alto horn for fifty cents at an auction. It was covered with green tarnish, and dented and kinked all over where old George had dropped it or fallen on it, but it still had a nice tone. Mellowed by countless jugs of Green River.

One of the last of the country bands in these parts was led by an eccentric recluse — I'll call him Bert — whose sole joy and hobby, aside from counting his reputed wealth, was band music. He finally gave it up when he lost his teeth, and his Sears Roebuck replacements would blow out whenever he tried to play his horn; but I saw him just the other day, standing outside his lonely farmhouse, and maybe he'll make it to the century mark.

Bert, though strictly self-taught, had one of the greatest possible assets for leading a country band: he was almost stone deaf. Once, at a concert, the music sheets had got mixed up, and we all began playing parts from different selections, in all sorts of keys and times. Everybody was blasting away for several minutes, and nobody noticed anything wrong until one player happened to look over at the title on his neighbor's music score.

They didn't have a piccolo player, so Bert used to bribe me to play at some of his engagements with an offer of free gasoline — maybe forty cents' worth — and coffee and doughnuts. I didn't have a piccolo of my own, and played a borrowed old six-holer with a crack plugged up with chewing gum and the keys held down with rubber elastics. . . .

Has there ever been a teenager who played some instrument, anything from a jewsharp to a bass tuba, who did not sometimes dream of becoming a professional? You're sitting up there on the stage of Symphony Hall, the conductor nods to you as the introduction ends; you stand up, and with perfect assurance, strike up the first movement of the most incredibly difficult concerto ever written by Shostakovich for the xylophone. And soon after, you're off on a concert tour of the capitals of Europe.

Well, I came pretty close. For a couple of years I occupied the first flute chair in the Keene High School orchestra, before my formal education — musical and otherwise — came to an abrupt end at seventeen. The great John Philip Sousa himself, on tour at the time with his band, once directed us in a performance of his *Stars And Stripes Forever*. When we got to the climactic piccolo obbligato, I managed to hit *almost* every note.

As for the capitals of Europe, years later I did play in one of them — Budapest. I was down there for a weekend, after a winter job skiing in Austria, doing some research on a legend I had heard to the effect that the red-haired Hungarian girls were the most beautiful in the world.

I happened to hear one of the best tzigane (gypsy) folk orchestras, playing at a restaurant, and was at once hypnotized by this strange wild music. Sometimes it came very close to the old square dance melodies of my youth. For three days I went to this nightspot every evening and stayed until dawn. My only instrument at the time was a battered and much-repaired clarinet I had picked up in Salzburg for eight dollars. But I found that if I slipped each of the five musicians a dollar — an American dollar was equal to ten in Hungary — they were very happy to have me sit in with them.

My last evening in Budapest, the tzigane leader, around midnight, silenced the crowd and made an announcement. A Hungarian friend translated it for me. "He says, he will now perform an imitation of the drunken American trying to play the clarinet."

Going back to the 1920's, I suppose one reason I continued to play square dance music, at least occasionally, was because this music was almost unknown among young people at that time. It gave me at least some sort of distinction, though I would then have been much happier if I could have played, half as well, either jazz or classical music. In those years I was often involved with some informal four-or-five piece orchestra, usually for fun, but sometimes to pick up a little extra money.

Such groups were brought to the farm in summer by my brother, who went to college and later worked in New York. To them our square dance music was a real novelty, but nobody ever took it seriously, including ourselves — it was considered just a sort of musical clowning act.

FAMILY ORCHESTRA

As some of our popular sentimental writers have it, the surviving native families of rural southern New Hampshire are simple, kindly folk, little touched by the world outside. They all get together at weekly square dances in the village hall, and skillfully whirl through the ancient quadrilles and contras, to the music of their ancestors played by some old native fiddler. The further removed from the truth such nonsense becomes, I guess, the better the market for it.

Actually there are many more numbers of people doing what they call square dancing, today, in the sub-urban areas around Boston and New York than in any remote country regions. Up here in our part of the world there is only one old fiddler still alive, within a hundred miles, with the knowledge and ability to play much of the genuine old music. He is in his eighties and hasn't played for dancing in some twenty-five years.

We attended a typical country dance, in one of our remote hill townships, last summer. The nearest thing to real square dance music we heard that evening was *On The Trail Of The Lonesome Pine*, played on a sax and an electric guitar, accompanied by deafening thunderclaps from a trap drummer whose style was copied from the Beatles. The only dancers were young people from a nearby summer colony.

Back in my prehistoric boyhood, suburbia was still a long way off. Most of the old social customs still prevailed. Every township had at least one so-called family orchestra, and I played sometimes with others besides our own. They ranged from professional calibre, like the New England Conservatory trained Peaveys down in Milford, to the most illiterate of backwoods performers. Only a few such groups, by the way, ever played square dance music. It was considered highly immoral by most churchpeople, and others looked down on it as being "unrefined."

Occasionally in winter we would make the two hour trip by horse and sleigh to the village hall in Stoddard, New Hampshire, a town even more primitive than our own. There we would join forces with the Holmes family and play for the square dancing. They played only by ear, but quite well, their own versions of the old tunes. One night, when we had just come inside the hall from an outside temperature of something like 25 below zero, my flute was soon coated with a thick layer of frosty ice, like a mint julep glass.

There were always a few jugs of hard cider passed around outside the Stoddard hall, and the dancing was pretty wild. Many of the characters who came out of the woods up there looked like the Mountain Men of frontier days. When a fist fight began in the back of the hall, the dancing and music went on without interruption.

Our own family orchestra was most active in summer. My brother and some cousins down the road would be home for vacation, and Cousin Percy would be in his cottage at the Farm. For an audience, we had the summer guests at the farmhouse, ten or a dozen families in the cottages around the Pond, and often most of the population from other nearby summer resorts, Travel to town was difficult in those days and there was little else to provide evening entertainment.

I remember one time when we still had the big old foot-powered parlor organ — hardly anyone owned a piano up here until later years — when a rather eccentric English writer, who was boarding at the Farm, took my father aside. This English chap, who had never been seen to smile, told my father he had a marvelously humorous idea. "Let us smuggle the melodeon down to the shore of the lake," he said, "And secrete it amongst the shrubbery. Then, in the evening, when darkness falls, someone will begin playing on it. It will be a huge joke, you know!"

Maybe my father was too busy to see the joke. Anyway, he said it would have taken six men to lug that goddam organ down to the lake and back.

For several years Cousin Percy directed most of our musical efforts, putting on elaborate concerts at the town hall for special occasions. And he continued to give me daily flute lessons until I was sixteen, but before then his mouse-brained wife had put a stop to his musical evenings at the Farm. "Why should you go down there and entertain all thothe thummer people for nothing, Perthy?" she would lisp.

Cousin Percy was a tall, thin, freckled, sandy-haired man with a face as narrow as tennis star Bill Tilden's and a similarly comparable style with a racket. (While earning his way through college, he had got letters in boxing, swimming and diving, and tennis, and excelled in dramatics.) His husky tenor voice was enormously expressive and usually sardonic. His closeness with money had become a legend in our family even before he married his penny-pinching wife. But unlike her, he would not stint on certain things that meant most to him; his fly rods and musical instruments were made to order and always the best; and he usually had a Cadillac-class car, which he would drive fifteen miles out of his way to find gas a cent or two below the usual price. Whenever some pipe smoker at the Farm showed an interest in the tobacco he used in his old corncob (cut plug which he shaved off with a jack-knife), Cousin Percy would ignore the empty pipe being held expectantly toward him, and remark, "You ought to try it — next time you're down to the village just ask for Everyday Light — costs eleven cents a plug." Then he would shove the remaining shavings of tobacco carefully into his pocket, and puffing away happily, stroll off toward his cottage.

When he married, Cousin Percy made no effort to conceal the fact that he had mainly been attracted by the half-million his bride would inherit. This materialized when he was thirty or so, and he at once retired, devoting the rest of his life to playing the flute, fishing, and memorizing every fall a complete statistical history of each of the major college football games. He also carried two black notebooks every day of his life, in which he jotted down, numbered and dated, every new story he heard; dirty in one book, clean in the other.

There had been a time when Cousin Percy often sat in with some symphony orchestra or large band. A fine clarinetist before he took up the flute, he was always welcomed because of the flawless precision of his playing. Every intricacy of harmony and rhythm was as familiar to him as the mathematics he had taught, before retiring, at Columbia. (He had also taught at Hawaii and in Japan, and was something of an expert on Polynesian music.)

As they grew older, his wife wouldn't come to their summer cottage any more, and she began to think of ways of keeping him always at home. They lived in two rooms in the rear of her big old family house in the city, the rest of which they rented "to save money." During his last several years, though somewhat crippled with arthritis, he continued to practice a few hours every day, locked up in his bedroom. And I suppose that in all those years nobody except his wife, who hated music, ever heard him play. He had long since mastered all the most difficult flute music available, and had taken to writing out even more intricate exercises for himself. He had never cared a damn about melody; it bored him, he claimed. But he always encouraged me to go on playing our old reels and hornpipes, because, he said,

23

they made "excellent exercises in articulation." I always felt that secretly he really enjoyed hearing them.

Sometime after Cousin Percy died, his widow asked me to come down to see her. Thinking about his fine Haynes flute and piccolos (always kept in perfect condition), I dropped whatever I was doing and drove the hundred miles in a hurry. He left no nearer relatives than myself, and she had almost none. But even if it should turn out I was only getting some of his voluminous collection of books of music for the flute, the trip would be well worthwhile.

As I drove along toward Manchester that day, many boyhood memories came back. Cousin Percy directing an Old Home Day concert of Hawaiian music — for weeks before, he had drilled our family orchestra, augmented by some twelve recruits from the summer colony, mostly playing ukeleles, mandolins, and guitars, and with several choral interludes. (At the last moment, he had recruited me, aged nine and scared to death, to play his flute parts, because one of his false front teeth had fallen out.) He had even taught a couple of the girls to do authentic hula dances. And all this was before the fad for Hawaiian music had begun in the United States, and the stuff had become a travesty.

I also reflected on a characteristic of Cousin Percy's which had been, back in those days, most rare among musicians. He hated what he called musical snobs. Over the years he had made us play anything and everything. Classical, opera, ragtime, jazz, square dance music, band marches. And whatever it was, we could never meet his exacting standards — the best we could do was what

24

he called "getting by," the kindest words he ever had for anyone he ever played with.

It was Cousin Percy who first told me that *The National Emblem* was a far better march than anything Sousa had ever composed. This piece, long nicknamed "The Monkey Wrapped His Tail Around The Flagpole," was written by an old bandleader named Bagley, down in Keene, our county seat, back about 1900 or before. He sold it outright for twenty dollars — it was, I guess, the only composition he ever sold — and he died without any idea of how popular it would become. It is today, as it has been for the past fifty years, the most often played, the world around, of any band march ever written.

Then there were the memories of those evenings, several times a week, when Cousin Percy would be down at the farmhouse playing with us just for the fun of it, and we would soon all be trying to attain standards we never approached before or after. If you played a note that wasn't at least technically correct, he would stop the whole outfit and we would have to start over again, with no regard at all for our audience. If the offender happened to be some summer guest sitting in with us, it made no difference. "Miss Brown, are you playing with us or against us?" he would ask, baring his china teeth in a fiendish grin. "If you don't have a good ear for music, get rid of your violin, and take up the victrola!" Poor Miss Brown often as not burst into tears and retired from the scene.

When I finally arrived at the old house, Cousin Percy's widow was so glad to see me she actually offered me a cup of coffee — without cream, of course. No flutes and no piccolos were in evidence. Doubtless she had spent a month taking them to every second-hand instrument dealer in New England to get the last penny out of them. Gone too was the music library. But with much sentiment and ceremony, she presented me with a stack of cheap, yellowed, music notebooks, containing the exercises Cousin Percy had composed.

The notebooks were all filled with his own peculiar scrawled musical notation, resembling at first glance the tracks of a hummingbird whose feet had been dipped in ink. Nobody on earth but the old flute player himself could ever possibly have read them. I accepted them with what I hoped would seem like heartfelt gratitude. But I suppose I already had the best thing he could have left me — some, at least, of the enduring benefits that could come only from such relentless teaching when I was very young.

In the summers shortly after Cousin Percy was no longer around at the Farm, another character who contributed much to our musicales was Mr. Hazard, an old gentleman in his eighties who had played in Sherman's band on the march to Georgia in the Civil War. He had become a concert violinist and led a large orchestra in New York for a time. Then he had gone into business and made a great deal of money, and he spent the last twenty-five years of his life happily pursuing his two great hobbies — fly fishing, and playing old square dance melodies on his Stradivarius violin. Mr. Hazard, who had first come up to try the fishing, was delighted to find that we, too, knew some of the authentic old jigs, reels, and hornpipes. And he taught me many more that we had not known.

In contrast to Cousin Percy, he was dedicated to attaining the utmost in melodic expression. He would drill me patiently, by the hour, on some simple tune like *The Devil's Dream,* trying to show me, in his always considerate, courteous way, that it could be played with all the finesse and delicacy that would be demanded in a rapid passage from a Beethoven concerto. He could play many of the difficult old tunes on two strings in harmony, and he taught me a great deal about how to arrange second parts properly for this sort of music.

Some of Mr. Hazard's serenity and patience may have resulted from his having become a Christian Scientist in his later years. But his tolerance left him at the mere mention of saxophones, then much in vogue. "Musical abortions," he called them. "A desecration and a perversion of that fine instrument, the clarinet . . . . there should be a *law,* like Prohibition, preventing their sale or use!" Whenever someone came along with a sax to play with us, the old gentleman would at once pack up his violin and depart.

Mr. Hazard was the first truly educated and accomplished musician I knew who had made square dance music his special province, and who fully realized much of its potential. But I didn't think much about the significance of this until some thirty years later.

There were several summers when we often got together with the Rice clan from nearby Dublin. They would come over ten strong, all piled into old Dr. Rice's big Pierce-Arrow. They were all singers and could put on a professional rendering of any Gilbert and Sullivan operetta, their family specialty, on a moment's notice. But the Doctor (a Tufts College dean who had lived in Dublin as a boy) liked best to play his fiddle with us. He knew the old tunes well, but delighted in trying to see how fast he could play them. And after several rounds of his home-made prescription, alcohol gin, his rotund face glowing like a polished Baldwin apple and his white mustache quivering, his bow would get to sawing away at such speed you couldn't even see it. Nobody could keep up with him, to his great satisfaction, on *Money Musk* and *Speed The Plow*.

Meanwhile Mrs. Rice, a quiet little woman who taught piano in the classical manner, would sip her gin, and remark happily to nobody in particular, "My darling Doctor is having *such* a good time!"

Our family orchestra was naturally most active back in those years before many of the summer people had cars, and the only canned music came from a squeaky hand-wound victrola. But my brother and I always continued playing the old tunes a few times a year, at family parties and occasional square dances. In time we were joined by our own children, who also grew up playing the same old music.

DARLING NELLIE GRAY

FOR THIRTY-FIVE YEARS, following the revival of square dancing in Nelson, New Hampshire, I never quite gave up hope that some day we would again play the fine old music. That somebody would come along who would care about it. Most of the time it remained a pretty forlorn hope.

Some of the time I played quite regularly for the Nelson dances, and for one stretch of four or five years hardly missed a Saturday night in the Nelson hall and also played now and then in most other southern New Hampshire towns. There were other intervals in which I hardly played at all from one year to the next.

In the late 1940's Janet, my dance loving wife, ran weekly square dances for a whole year in the town hall, while I managed the music — usually two or three hired hands and myself. Our purpose, besides providing entertainment for the local young people and having some fun, was to raise enough money to spruce up the old hall. It had seen no new paint in its smoke-darkened interior since around the time of the Civil War.

The Puritanical town fathers had never approved of dancing, and when presented with our hard-earned cash at the end of the year, simply put it all into the general fund, leaving the hall as it was. So the joke was on us, though at the moment we didn't see the humor of the situation. Anyway, for a long time afterward, I had had enough of playing for square dances.

The experience of that year, so far as the music was concerned, had been little fun and a great deal of hard work and frustration. And in fact, during the whole time from 1930 to 1965, I almost never got to play any of the fine old melodies I had learned in younger days. Nor was anyone else playing them. We could never find any musicians who knew them, or any callers who would use them. Square dance music, to New England square dance enthusiasts, and to the world at large, seemed to be irrevocably represented by tunes like *Darling Nellie Gray, Redwing,* and Polish polkas.

In the early 1930's, two main factors led to the sudden revival of square dancing, a revival in which Nelson became something of a center. First, many former summer people and other city dwellers moved up to the country permanently after the 1929 crash, and when they got here they began looking for "country" customs. And second, the weekend skiers began to arrive on the scene — the White Mountain ski resorts were not yet developed to any extent.

Old natives like my father and mother, who hadn't set foot on a dance floor since they were young, found themselves in great demand to teach the newcomers all the fine points of the traditional figures and how to follow the calls.

But most of the old-time "prompters" still living were too feeble to last long. A new breed, the "singing callers," were soon flourishing far and wide. Music to them was incidental; all they wanted was a strong beat and something to accompany their singing. It was a technique that depended very largely on that new invention, the microphone.

Let any singing caller get his hand on a mike, and he would be off and away, drunk with the power of his own voice, while some illiterate fiddlers would be droning away in the background. The musicians were never allowed a mike of their own (they would have drowned out the caller's warbling) which, considering the kind of music they played, was probably just as well.

Albert Quigley, our local fiddler with whom I played on and off for some thirty years, and who knew some good old tunes but seldom got a chance to play them, went so far as to blame the degeneracy of modern square dance music entirely on the advent of singing calls. But Quig was somewhat biased. He firmly believed, as he often told me, that "all square dance callers have a screw loose somewhere — it's a necessary part of their trade."

We had one caller for two or three seasons who was actually a pretty fair singer, but soon got the obsession that the dancers came mainly to hear him perform. His theme song was *Darling Nellie Gray*, which he always used for the last dance of the evening, and we would have to play it, over and over, for about twenty minutes, while he displayed his vocal virtuosity. Even if one had loved *Darling Nellie Gray* to begin with, after a year or so of that weekly routine, it would have been nice not to have to listen to it for quite awhile. Forever, so far as I'm concerned.

Quig's reaction to callers was typical of most musicians who had to work with them. In the old days, dances had been a purely social activity; no profit motive, beyond sometimes passing the hat for a hard-working volunteer group of musicians. But when square dances began to be revived, they were at once commercialized, like most everything else in this materialistic era. Somebody — it might be the caller himself, or just anyone with an eye for making a few bucks — would lease the hall, hire two or three musicians, and advertise weekly dances, admittance one dollar or whatever.

Naturally the profits depended largely on the amount that had to be paid to the musicians. Most callers hired their own musicians — the rock-bottom, cheapest talent that could be found. I played with many groups during the depression years when we were happy to get two or three dollars each for an evening's work. The caller might clear ten for himself, after expenses. (If there was a poor crowd, he might just say, hard luck, boys, no pay tonight, better luck next week!) Hence it was rare to find any great amount of love between musicians and callers — a relationship existing in most square dance groups ever since.

And so, as square dancing continued to spread throughout New England in the 1930's, it was in spite of the accompanying music generally heard. While we were thought to have better music in Nelson than in many other places, I can only say that even with my long-toughened ears, I could usually get through the evening only by making frequent trips to the woodshed, where we kept a bottle of some appropriate anaesthetic handy.

As for the new generation of square dancers, they had never heard any authentic old music, and so accepted whatever was being played without protest. Anyway they generally made so much noise themselves, they couldn't hear it.

One thing that made playing with almost any square dance band bearable, was the great good fellowship of my fellow artists. Whatever their musical shortcomings, they were great people to know, and I made many lasting friendships among them. Even if I had wanted to treat their playing in a patronizing manner, I was hardly in any position to do so. I never had time to practice, hadn't read a note of music since school days, and was usually blowing on some borrowed, battered sax or whatever. (My old silver flute was stolen at a dance in the mid-Thirties, and it was many years before I could afford another.) And when it came time to play *Darling Nellie Gray* I could murder it as thoroughly as anybody else.

One colorful character who comes to mind was a not-very-well-self-taught drummer, Buddy Brown, whose main vocation was driving a huge old ten-wheeler logging truck. We would have been happier without the drums, but there was a winter when the only caller we could find was an old fellow who worked with Buddy, so we had to hire them both.

Buddy was a rugged, red faced, jolly man who must have weighed around two hundred and fifty, in his late forties. His silent little blond wife always came with him, looking sad eyed and underfed.

At intermission, Buddy would hurry out with a big fat girl who would be waiting for him at the door, and they would disappear into the pinewoods beyond the hall. They were never back when the music began again, and Buddy's wife would climb up on the stage and start patiently pumping the foot-pedal on the bass drum. Before long, Buddy would have driven away with the fat girl in her car.

After the dance, Buddy's wife would pack up his drums and lash them onto the logging truck, climb into the cab and warm up the engine, and roar off alone into the snowy night.

Our musicians were not always rustic or lacking in real talent. We had one of the best banjo players I ever heard, a young law student who needed the money; a little clarinet player who had drunk his way up to some top name bands and all the way down again and played everything, even our darling Nellie, in the style of Benny Goodman; and for some years, a fine bass player whom we had never seen touch even a beer, who dropped dead one night of acute alcoholism. And there were others, but none of them knew many of the traditional melodies, nor did they have any conception of the traditional manner of playing them.

A caller who had much to do with the revival of square dancing in Nelson was Ralph Page, a local boy a little older than myself. But Ralph soon became a full-time professional and left the Nelson scene for more lucrative jobs. The best known and most successful of New England callers, he has performed all around the United States and made several tours abroad.

Page and my first wife, Beth Tolman, wrote *The Country Dance Book,* illustrated by my brother, Fran. Published in New York by A. S. Barnes Company, it went through many editions and remains a basic authority on square dance technique.

Quig, who played the fiddle for Page and others for some twenty-five years, also lived in Nelson, and also incidentally was a fine landscape painter and an expert frame maker. In his later years he seldom played here, as he needed more steady employment than Nelson had been providing. He had long since become convinced, as I had, that the old authentic music would never be heard again at any public square dance. Melodies like some of those he knew from his boyhood, and had been able to play brilliantly in younger days.

For my own part, by 1950 or so, I never expected to play again for square dances. And for a dozen years I was much too busy with other things to think about music at all. My flute was seldom touched except when Janet lifted it to dust off the top of the piano.

And so we come to the beginning, six or seven years ago, of what might be called the second revival of square dancing in Nelson. A happening in which the music itself becomes the dominant factor.

SQUARE AND FOLKSY

A NEW YOUNGER GENERATION had grown up taking square dances for granted. Just something you could go to, in almost any town in southern New Hampshire, on Friday or Saturday night, if there was nothing else to do. In many places, so-called Western style dancing had supplanted the older New England contra dances, and the music could be anything so long as it had a fast beat, often coming from a record-player.

The "second revival" of square dancing — and the renaissance of authentic old music — began on our local scene with the arrival of Dudley Laufman. He started calling when only eighteen or so, and got some jobs doing social work up at the State institution for the insane. (Quig would have said an ideal background for a square dance caller.)

Dudley Laufman was a far different type than the rustic and pseudo-rustic callers, some of them musically illiterate, we had had to employ a few years earlier. He could only have been a product of this newly emerging national folk-music scene. A self-styled poet and ardent practitioner of the "natural" life, he and his young wife built a picturesque one-room cabin out of various odds and ends, near the old Shaker village of Canterbury, New Hampshire. The place at once became a rendez-vous for the "folksy people" from all over. The family — there were in due course two or three kids — was precariously supported by Dudley's calling engagements, sometimes as far away as Boston or Cambridge. During especially lean times, a vegetable patch and some goats kept them from starvation.

Dudley became interested in Nelson's illustrious his-tory as one of the principal centers involved in the ear-lier revival of square dancing. Soon he began to pick up the old authentic music — such of it as we could remem-ber — and began re-creating the old dance forms, dis-pensing entirely with the waltzes, polkas, and modern dances which in recent years were generally intermixed with squares at most public dances.

Among Dudley's devotées were the usual wild-haired, barefoot girls carrying guitar cases which probably held nothing but their spare underwear, and there were bearded characters who twanged away on home-made zithers. But the types who interested me were a new breed of square dance musicians altogether — neither strictly professionals nor in any sense dilettantes. Like some of the old people I had known so long ago, when I was small, they seemed to like our music entirely for its own sake, and they worked hard to master it and get the most out of it.

There were almost as many musicians attracted to our

square dance revival as there were dancers, and it wasn't long before I found myself prodded into playing once again. Sometimes there would be ten or a dozen amateurs with their fiddles, flutes, or whatnot, all crowding up onto our little stage, anxious to learn the old tunes nobody had cared about back in the days of our earlier revival, when the dancing itself had been the only interest.

Dudley to be sure acquired a following of dancers from far and wide — many from the Boston area, some from as far away as central Vermont. Not all young, incidentally; a number were middle aged and some older. The fact that these people were willing to drive from 75 to 150 miles, each way, to attend the dances, speaks for itself. Certainly nothing quite like this had ever happened before.

In the old days the caller would go out and get himself a nice rest, and maybe a drink or two, between squares. But Dudley decided it would be one square after another, right through the evening — and soon the crowd came to expect it that way. Such continuous playing requires considerable stamina; especially when, for fifteen minutes or so at a time, we play something like *Ladies' Walpole Reel* or *Chorus Jig* which if done properly demand the utmost in precision and expression. This has quickly been discovered by one or another symphony players who thought it would be fun to sit in with us.

Dudley was much given to using — at one period of his career — melodies he had acquired through his association with the more precious of the folksy-music

38

groups and clubs in the Cambridge-Boston area. The kind of simple tunes we would expect to hear at suburban conclaves of English Morris Dance enthusiasts. A favorite of his was a rather sickly thing entitled *Mutual Love*. One evening I reached for the mike and announced to the waiting dancers that we were about to play Mutual Fornication. Thereafter, as Dudley frequently reminded me, it was a case of put up or shut up.

Another of our caller's idiosyncracies (which he still employs now and then) was to keep the band in suspense while he got all the dancers lined up and explained the figures to them. Then, and only then, he would turn to us and say, "Go ahead, boys — let's have *Ross's Reel Number Four* in F!" If anybody didn't know *Ross's Reel*, or couldn't remember how it begins, it was just too bad. The piano had started banging out a chord, the dance had begun, and we were off. This method, Dudley would explain, gives our music a more "spontaneous character."

The focus on Dudley here is not so much because he is lately thought by many to be the ablest caller and square dance teacher in New England, but rather because he has played such a large part in the development of our music. Though I may have accorded him less flattering titles at one time or another, he has really been our catalyst. It was he, and his followers, who made it possible to revive the dances in the Nelson town hall. The dances in turn became a rallying place for musicians from far and near who wanted to play, or at least to hear, our old music. Students of this sort of music have brought us old books and manuscripts and scores

39

collected in Ireland, Scotland, Canada and elsewhere — literally thousands of melodies. Also many tapes and recordings.

Many excellent instrumentalists — both from the symphonic and the popular fields — began coming up here to try a hand at playing with us. In fact, hardly a week goes by these days without someone of this sort appearing at our door, so we haven't exactly been working just by ourselves in a musical vacuum. We've had much encouragement, not to mention a free education in modern instrumental techniques, from our professional visitors. Most have not hesitated to admit that playing the old music, as it was intended to be played, was not something they could accomplish without a fair measure of hard work and practice.

Meanwhile we continue to perform, once a month or so, in the old Nelson town hall with Dudley and his unique following. At the last dance, I counted eighteen musicians, at some point in the evening, all playing — a sort of square dance symphony. It was probably the largest ensemble to be heard playing that sort of music, in a New England town hall, in close to a century. And in contrast to the motley crew who used to appear only a few years ago, all of these people were well trained, and some of them were very expert performers.

Who are all these musicians who have been up here in southern New Hampshire playing all this nebulous old music? Are they really good musicians? What are their names? For the musical snob who is looking for big names and glittering portraits on expensive record albums, there won't be much satisfaction. And by musical snobs, I mean some of your best friends and mine — not really snobs in any other sense — just not conditioned to respond to any music unless it carries a familiar label; who never quite dare trust their own reactions.

But, let's see, not to leave our friends completely frustrated, at one point I counted among our various musicians: an air-force pilot recently turned contractor; a Harvard psychiatrist; a philosophy professor at an upstate college; an electronics engineer; the proprietor of a crafts shop; a poet turned sandalmaker; and a writer; and some others I've forgotten. People who care about music well-played — and the hell with the promotion — who have found some music that was lost for a long time and have had the good fortune to bring it back to life.

As for most of the well-known names in the lucrative and popular field known as "country music," I had friends as far back as the 1920's who were singing, and composing, so-called cowboy ballads — and had never seen a horse outside of Central Park. There is not now, nor has there ever been, any such thing as genuine "country music."

Consequently I was amused at the reaction of a contemporary conductor-composer, at a party where we played some things arranged by Niel Gow, famous musician of Edinburgh and London in the late eighteenth century. I was talking to someone from the audience afterwards, when the conductor passing by with a knowledgable smile, remarked over his shoulder, "Oh, yes, country music. . . ." So far as he was concerned, we might as well have been playing *Old Joe Clark* on electric guitars and a musical saw.

Recently two young people from New York, or was it Philadelphia, armed with fine Haynes piccoloes, sat in with us for an evening in Nelson. So I got out my own, and we did a couple of things in harmony, with three piccoloes (One more than you're likely to hear in the Boston Symphony). Several interested listeners afterward asked me who our piccolo-playing friends were, but I hadn't caught their names. Whoever they were, they had played our music very well, and if they should come again sometime, maybe we might find out what their names were.

WE MADE THE BIG-TIME.
ONCE.

WE HAD REACHED A POINT, in our Nelson dances, where
several musicians were appearing fairly regularly from
widely separated places in New Hampshire, Vermont,
and Massachusetts. One day, now some years ago, we
each received an excited note from Dudley Laufman,
saying he had got us booked to play a concert number
at the forthcoming first Newport Folk Festival. Fame
and fortune at last!

At the time, Dudley himself hadn't laid any great
claim to musicianship. While calling to some of the
more simple tunes, he would sometimes wheeze out a
few rudimentary chords on an old accordion. When
still very young, he told us one night he was going to
take a trip to Ireland, and as he had no money at all,
planned to play and sing every night for his lodging.
"Don't do it," I advised him. "Why not?" he demanded.
"Well, the first night you try it, somebody will shoot
you." Some of Dudley's friends thought this was terribly
unkind of me. But I claimed it probably saved his life.

Years later he did go to Ireland, with his wife, but I don't think he played for their lodgings. Instead, he took a camera to make illustrations for his book of Irish-inspired poetry.

Other talents aside, Dudley is nothing short of a genius as a backwoods impressario. He had somehow managed to land us on the opening spot on Saturday night at Newport, when we were still so unorganized nobody knew just who, or how many of us, would be playing. We had never once rehearsed as a group, and we didn't even have a name.

Our repertoire of the authentic old melodies was still very limited. Perhaps half a dozen first-class scores that all of us knew well enough to attempt together, and not likely to be known by any other performers.

None of us showed the slightest enthusiasm about going to Newport and nobody seemed especially flattered, as I recall it, except Dudley himself. He assured us the engagement would overnight bring us lucrative contracts; Columbia Records, television, and whatnot. But what persuaded us, mainly, was just the prospect of a free weekend at the seashore.

We decided our ambitious leader should book us as "The Canterbury Country Orchestra" for want of a more accurate title. Only Dudley himself came from Canterbury.

I would have been much happier with several rehearsals, but we could never get the crowd together for any such formal preparation. Finally most of us managed to have one brief session. About all we had time to do was decide on what numbers we would play. It would have to be by ear, of course. We had little in the way of scores in those days, and anyway two or three of the group couldn't read music.

We had all read or heard about the crowds and the wild times occasioned by the Jazz Festivals. But we knew nothing at all about this newly invented Folk Festival. We envisioned a couple of hundred people sitting out in a field, listening to some characters under an apple tree, singing and twanging on guitars.

Instead we found ourselves climbing up onto a huge elevated stage, with a sea of faces below stretching off into the distance and out of sight. (Next morning we learned there had been sixteen thousand admissions; more than at the Jazz Festival, but the Folksy crowd had caused no riots nor much commotion — they just *looked* wild. Too bad it all got out of hand in later years.)

While we milled around on the stage trying to get into position and remember what we were supposed to play, Dudley started shouting into his mike. It seemed he wanted to make sure the audience wouldn't think we were an illiterate hillbilly band.

We would begin, he said, with *Money Musk,* while some friends who had come with us would illustrate the figures of the dance as we played. And acting on a sudden inspiration, he added that as an introduction, we had a young fellow from home who could play *Money Musk* as a slow strathspey in the seventeenth-century Scottish mode; after which we would all launch into it at a fast contra-dance tempo. "Step right up here," he said, handing a fiddle to the startled Fred, who was one of the dance group but not a regular member of the orchestra.

Fred had been sitting in the rear wings drinking beer, and probably thought this was just some sort of rehearsal. All he could see was the blinding glare from the lights. He walked up to the mike and started sawing away, but in the middle of the first strain he missed a note. "Oh, shit!" he said, and stopped. "Well, it don't matter, I'll start over again." This time he got through it without a hitch, and the applause was deafening.

Afterward, when I told Fred there had been sixteen thousand people out there, he turned white, and I thought he was going to faint.

We didn't play anything very exciting that night, and I didn't think we played very well. But our little concert drew a big hand. Joan Baez danced into a front row seat and said she thought the music was great. (I've admired Baez ever since, and hope to hear her sing sometime.)

We had fine writeups in the Sunday newspapers next day. One imaginative reporter described us as having the shortest hair, by far, of any group in the entire festival, while playing what was probably the most "authentic" of all the music heard that evening.

Offstage at Newport, we mingled happily with all the hairy performers, African folk groups, and other characters. One of Dudley's camp-followers, a big friendly tangle-haired girl, on finding my wife was not there, got in free by writing my name with "Mrs." on her identification badge. I told her that considering my age, and one thing and another, it would probably be just as well if she didn't carry out this ploy to the point where, on reaching our assigned quarters, we might end up sharing a double bed.

Together with a large and varied assortment of our fellow artists, we were luxuriously billeted in a huge old mansion by the sea. Back there after the show, in a great drawing room, many of us played and drank oceans of free beer until sunrise.

Following its triumphal Newport debut, the Canterbury Country Orchestra kept on more in name than in actuality; except for frequent sitting-in of some of the members here in Nelson, where we don't bother with names anyway. Dudley managed to round us up a few times to play at a Cambridge coffee shop called Club 47. And we also played two or three times at the annual Beers Family festivals at Fox Hollow, in Petersburg, New York.

Bob Beers and his family live on an old and remote country estate with a vast expanse of open pasture and fields. The place is said to have been the hang-out of the Prohibition-days gangster, Legs Diamond, until he was gunned down by a rival. On a weekend, every August, the genial and rotund Mr. Beers is host to a great horde of best-known, slightly-known, and (not without good reason) completely unknown of the folk music performers from everywhere.

The Beerses themselves are old pros, celebrated for their playing of ancient instruments and singing — concert tours, recordings, and television shows. But it was my impression, at least for the first few summers, that the Fox Hollow festivals were not at all commercially inspired. Profits all went toward maintaining the camp grounds and stage, and paying expenses. It's Bob Beers' idea of how to have a great good time.

Hundreds of performers, and also some of the thousands who pay to attend the evening concerts, camp out in a sort of tent city spread all over the pastures. Below, in the woods, a large well equipped raised stage faces a natural amphitheatre. The audience sits on the ground beneath a canopy of lofty treetops.

The last time I went over to Fox Hollow (the affair has since got too big and too crowded for my liking) a heavy shower held up the show. Finally, when it went on pouring steadily and everybody was pretty well soaked, they decided to cancel the rest of the evening program. But such is the die-hard enthusiasm of the folk fanatics, they wouldn't leave. Huddled under raincoats, ponchoes, blankets, or anything they could find, they persuaded Bob Beers to rally the performers.

By the time we were called upon, it was about three o'clock in the morning. During that evening, I had made a number of round trips to our tent up the hill, escorting various musicians and friends who seemed in some danger of chills. We had brought along a jug of bourbon for just such emergencies. And of course, every trip up the hill on one of these errands of mercy, I took a nip myself to make sure our guests would feel at ease.

As a result of all this traveling up and down from our tent, and the lateness of the hour, I had to be awakened from a sound sleep when we were announced.

As we climbed the stage, we decided hurriedly to play *Chorus Jig* — a well-worn dance tune all of us would be most likely to remember — under the circumstances.

One chap, who was backing me up with a second flute, wasn't quite sure — or so it seemed to me — what we were playing, or in what key it was. He wandered around the stage, giving out with some wild, piercing notes here and there, as he tried to find the microphone.

We got through it somehow, though everybody kept speeding up, rather like a record-player that had lost its governor. Had it not been for Kay Gilbert at the piano, our only sober performer, I'm sure we would have ended up at a tempo well beyond the sound barrier.

This masterpiece can still be heard, if anybody is interested, on a Beers recording (Fox Hollow Records.) We had not suspected we were being thus immortalized, together with a dozen or two other performers, most of whose musical accomplishments were of dubious quality. At least it can be said, on this record, our band is by far the most spirited.

Sometime before the year of our Newport adventure, I had become a member of the orchestra which is assembled once a year to play square dance music, both concert and dancing, at the spring New England Folk Festival. It is the one big away-from-home engagement (one afternoon and two evenings of playing) which I still thoroughly enjoy.

This began when Jack O'Connor, a young chap who had played with us several times at Nelson, became the music director for the Festival. My old Nelson neighbor,

Ralph Page, had long been the Festival's most famous caller. But I had never attended because, during the earlier years of this affair, I was seldom playing at all and had no hope that the great old square dance music of my youth could ever be revived.

The Festival promised a little real folding money, and April is when we're quite sure to be more broke than usual. But what lured me most that first year was the music scores Jack mailed me — imagine, playing some of our old tunes from written, prearranged scores! I hadn't looked at a note of music since high school days.

As it turned out, the Festival, held that year in the Armory over at Manchester, New Hampshire, was a vastly surprising experience. In this most commercial of all possible worlds, here was something different. Certainly the least publicized, least exploited, of any such large public gathering in all of New England. The place was packed, but my impression was that many who attended were also participants in some aspect of the program. Hundreds belonged to the many-costumed ethnic dance groups. Others were crafts exhibitors, amateur musicians, or worked on the food program.

Best of all, you could eat yourself to death for a dollar or so, exclusively on fare that a gourmet would have to travel around the world to find. Long tables, each loaded with all the special delicacies of a particular nation, each trying to outdo the others. The tough part was making a decision — a Swedish dinner, or perhaps Hungarian or Greek or Scottish, or should it be an Indonesian feast cooked over a charcoal brazier while you wait?

The regular festival orchestra led off with concert medleys of square dance music. Then we played at times for various guest callers, whatever tunes they asked for, and also for the general square dancing for all comers. During most of the ethnic dance exhibitions, using their own musicians or recordings, we managed to rest.

In succeeding years, the Festivals have been held in whatever Massachusetts towns might afford the largest high school buildings and parking areas, and they are always jammed to overflowing. Each year the quality of the orchestra has improved. Much more of our own authentic music has been added, lately using the *Nelson Music Collection* as a source; quite a thrill for Kay Gilbert and myself. Gone and unmourned is most of the standard pre-renaissance fare (*Trail of the Lonesome Pine, Beer Barrel Polka, Hinky Dinky Parlez-Vous.*)

Last year we did a concert number with the orchestra numbering twenty-four musicians. This was by far the largest orchestra ever to play square dance music in the United States in the present century. One old guest caller from another part of the country, weeping with joy, told us he had never expected to live long enough to hear such a great sound!

Thinking back to Newport — and the enthusiastic reception to our music there — it must have been in spite of our then very ragged performance. I'm sure it was the character of the music itself that appealed. It did not, at least, fit the public concept of what square dance music was expected to sound like. To that audience, it was a strictly new sound.

WHAT IS GOOD
SQUARE DANCE MUSIC?

WRITING ABOUT THE TRUE CHARACTER and value of good square dance music is a little like telling the folks back home all about that terrific show you saw in New York last week. But so many people ask us, these days, to explain what makes our music "different" from whatever they've heard elsewhere, it seems almost an obligation to try to give an answer in some detail.

Not to imply, however, that this is going to sound like some erudite essay on the embellishments of 15th century madrigals as compared to the original cantus firmus. Plain English will do well enough, and the hell with trying to impress some imaginary musical elite.

It may help to begin with a few thoughts about what our square dance music is *not,* before going on to explain what it *is.*

It happens that recently during one week there were three major shows on television, each of which featured an elaborate square dance extravaganza. The kind of shows on which the amount of money spent must be astronomical. Obviously the dance groups were recruited from the best professional talent in the country. And in all three shows, the dance numbers were superb, though of course not traditional except in a general way — all kinds of ballet tricks and elaborations, but very good dancing, naturally.

Doubtless each of these productions had employed a squad of the most expensive music specialists to provide the scores. What impressed me was how lousy the results were, compared to what could have been done with *good,* authentic square dance melodies. (It occurred to me that even without the music, the dancing would have been well worth watching; but it would be hard to imagine that anybody would want to listen to the music, by itself, for one minute.)

The dance act of the first show, an Irish style thing, began with the first strain of some common Irish jig. From there on, the composers had improvised their own conception of what Irish jigs should sound like: *diddle-de-diddle-de, diddle-de-diddle-de.* It could have been a parody, if it hadn't been so totally dull and characterless. Old man Beethoven did better with his ridiculous elaborations on Irish themes. (See Chapter Eight.)

In the second show, the choreography was based on the so-called western style of square dancing, and the music was equally dismal. The composers had chosen *Devil's Dream* (not the most interesting of reels) and repeated a bastard version of this tune, over and over and over. It was little more than just a beat.

The third show featured black performers, dancing a splendid quadrille. And this time the music was actually announced: *Turkey In The Straw*. I couldn't help suspecting that the Broadway producers, and the black cast, didn't know that *Turkey In The Straw* is another name for *Old Zip Coon*. This began as a minstrel show clog-dance number, back in the days when lampooning "the darkies" was done to a point that would make the Amos 'n' Andy series look highly flattering. (My earliest version is dated 1851.) And incidentally, *Old Zip Coon* is not only a fake square dance tune — it isn't a very good tune anyway, either for dancing or for listening. The most fitting place for it is in The Beginner's Instruction Book For The Banjo.

One more similar tune should be mentioned here, because its simple phrases must be by now about as familiar to the public as *America The Beautiful*. This is *The Arkansas Traveler,* used endlessly by show-business music writers and so-called country music artists on television and recordings.

After the Civil War, the tune was popularized in a well known vaudeville monologue. A man comes out on the stage with a fiddle and tells an interminable tale about being lost on horseback in Arkansas, near dark on a rainy night, and he finally comes to a ramshackle cabin. On the porch an old fellow is playing a fiddle. (Plays first strain of *Arkansas Traveler,* over and over.) Traveler interrupts him, asks for lodging, is refused, and old man plays same strain again. This goes on and on, with a series of side-splitters like

"Say, old man, why don't you shingle that leaky roof?"

"When it rains I can't and when it don't, there ain't no need to."

At last the exasperated traveler says "Why don't you play the second part of that tune?"

"Didn't know there was a second part."

Traveler takes fiddle and plays second strain. Old man jumps up, invites traveler inside, beds and feeds his horse, puts kettle on stove, tells traveler he's welcome to stay a week. Curtain.

I admit to some bias whenever I hear that particular tune. When I was small, I often had to provide the fiddle parts on my flute, while my older brother gave the monologue. But obviously *The Arkansas Traveler* came straight from Tin Pan Alley, and does not belong in any repertoire of traditional square dance music.

When we found ourselves getting seriously involved in collecting and playing square dance music, we began to specialize entirely in what we call jigs, reels, and hornpipes. We decided that clogs, polkas, schottisches, ballads and most other forms of folk music, had little more relevance to our field than jazz or the 12-tone scale. Then as we went on, we found three more old forms — strathspeys, rants, and planxtys — some of which we included as a sort of sub-species of our jigs or reels.

It seems that just about all the musical idioms of our western culture, excepting religious music, were originally designed for dancing of some sort. But in nearly every case — the minuet, the waltz, jazz, rock, or whatever — soon after being established, the idiom would be taken up by many musicians who played for listening rather than for dancing. So each idiom would eventually become a type of concert music, and be played as such forever afterward, while the original dance form might be quite forgotten.

There were literally many thousands of jigs, reels, and hornpipes, used for dancing in the past, and handed down to us in collections assembled indiscriminately. But our main interest is finding melodies which had enough intrinsic quality, or were especially composed or rearranged, to be enjoyed as "listening music" back in the Golden Age of such music.

It should be remarked, however, that of those melodies which were actually composed (especially from 1775 to 1850) for certain high-society occasions in London or Edinburgh, few seem to have much quality as we replay them today. Usually much better are those more ancient, time-tested classics of folk music — sometimes refined and adapted to the newer instruments and techniques of the period — whose origins are really unknown.

One rule of thumb has been perhaps of more value than our own musical judgement and analysis. We began to notice that after playing at some gathering, certain melodies would always be remembered. Perhaps a whole year later, somebody would come along and say, how about playing that jig again, you know, the one you played for us last year at such-and-such place . . . etc., etc. And again, a musician friend would write to ask us for a copy of the score of some melody that had evidently made some special appeal.

To put it another way, we have done our evaluating and selecting largely with a view toward the appeal of the music to present-day listeners, and the enjoyment it can afford to those who play it. Occasionally we find a tune of comparatively recent origin that we think is worthwhile. And though it has been helpful to know something of the history and technical nature of the music, I don't think it helps much to try to discover who composed, or who first wrote down, each specific melody, and exactly where and when.

So we aren't trying to pose as musical historians. Most of our research has been aimed at getting a better understanding of how the music can best be played. But in music scores, antiquity is no sign either of authenticity or of quality (though many recent folk music faddists don't seem aware of this fact.) Certainly some of the oldest music is also among the world's worst. Throughout the eighteenth and nineteenth centuries, the older tunes in square dance music were often being plagiarized, imitated, and aborted, by musicians and music publishers.

The reason much of the best square dance music we have was printed between 1750 and 1850, most likely, is because during that period some of the best musicians were playing it, employed by the richest and most discriminating patrons of the social world. It was also during that period that most musical instruments were redesigned and perfected much as we know them today, and afforded greatly improved techniques in playing. But at the same time a great amount of very poor stuff was also printed. I suppose just because there was so much of it, a lot more worthless stuff than good was handed down to us.

This may explain in part the almost totally unselective character of the collections of so-called old square dance music which have been printed in this century — whether in this country or in Canada or in the British Isles. In most of these collections, you can find the same basic tune repeated up to half a dozen times, under different names, with slightly differing arrangements. Usually there are many misprints, which probably got by because the publishers hadn't enough knowledge of the idiom to see how misplaced they obviously were. One wrong note can spoil the whole, as in most other music. (Except for typically *modern* compositions, in which if any note sounds right, you know it must be a misprint.)

JIGS

To get on with a brief discussion of each of the six categories of our square dance music, we'll begin with the jigs. *Jig, giga, gigue, gighardo.* . . . According to the Music Lover's Encyclopedia, "A light, brisk dance in 6/8 or 12/8 time." They didn't waste much time on that definition, did they?

I discussed this matter of how to properly describe a jig with Kay Gilbert, my talented and long-suffering accompanist and collaborator. (She drew, by hand, all the scores in our recently published *Nelson Music Collection*, some of which are reprinted in this book.) We got into quite an argument.

I began it by saying that the best authentic old jigs, usually in 6/8 time and occasionally in 9/8, sound rather like greatly speeded-up waltzes. Kay said this was technically inaccurate and misleading. I said maybe so, but it will do well enough for readers who are musically untrained, and the musically trained people shouldn't need to be told anyway.

I guess the best way is just to omit all such technical aspects of jigs as the use of diatonics, double tonics, or gin and tonics. The scores in these pages will have to speak for themselves.

As for the history of jigs — ages before written notes were devised, if we had a way of getting back there, we might find jigs being twanged on a one-string harp or whistled on a reed pipe. There may be some reason to think that this is the oldest set form of instrumental melody which has survived to the present day.

Many years ago, before much ethnic music had been recorded, I happened to hear some Macedonian folk-dance tunes. Greek friends told me they had been played for at least 2,000 years in their mountain villages. I was surprised to find a couple of the melodies, almost note for note, were identical to Irish jigs we played for square dancing and which had been brought over here in Colonial times by Irish settlers. The Irish probably had evolved their jigs from an ancient musical form known as the tarantella, brought to Ireland by sailors from the Mediterranean.

Musicologists and composers have condescendingly dismissed the jig as being something merely light, rollicking, or rapid. This may be acceptable, as applying to a passage in a longer work. But the description is hardly adequate in discussing traditional jigs, complete and separate entities in themselves. For the fascination of jigs lies in their great variety, despite the generally limited and fixed number of measures, Some typify the wildest and gayest of all musical idioms; others are extremely sad, delicate, and haunting.

From Beethoven's time to the present, all those who have assumed that all Irish jigs should sound much alike, have simply been ignorant of the basic nature of this music and unaware of how it could be played to best advantage.

Like a rapid passage in a difficult violin concerto, a good jig can merit no end of polishing — diminuendo and crescendo, smooth slurring here and staccato there, emphasis of certain key notes and phrases. About the only thing you must not do, in the way of expression, is to play a jig more slowly than its inherent natural tempo implies. The slightest lag in tempo can kill the best of jigs.

Playing too fast is just as bad. The usual "country music" style of racing through jigs is as abrasive to the eardrums as a record player with a broken speed regulator.

One last comment on jigs: If a tune sounds like *The Irish Washerwoman* or *St. Patrick's Day In The Morning* (thousands are more or less of this general type) we pass it by. But whenever we discover something like, for example, *The Brisk Young Lads,* or *Coleraine,* or *Humours of Glen,* we think we've struck gold. For any one of such melodies may be played an endless number of times, without ever playing it quite the same way twice.

PLANXTYS

Planxty is a handy word to throw out whenever you're

cornered by people who like to show off their musical erudition. It really throws them. If they go to look it up, they find most dictionaries don't include it. One standard music reference book suggests it is of Welsh origin. But this seems a bit odd, considering there is no *x* in the Welsh alphabet.

The planxty was an ancient form of dance. The tunes may be in any time, and vary in length. The best we have found resemble old jigs, but with the difference that the number of measures may not follow a set form. The second strain is often twice the length of the first.

So far we have found only about half a dozen planxtys that we feel have enough melodic interest to be worth playing.

STRATHSPEYS

Strathspeys are especially beloved and cherished by Scottish folk music buffs, and there are fiddlers who specialize in what they call the strathspey technique. At its best it can be very good. The extremely tricky grace notes derive from the skirling of pipes.

There are so many collections of strathspeys, ancient, intermediate, and modern, it would take a year to play through all of them. Unfortunately most are so imitative you can hardly tell one from another. One traditional form of strathspey begins at a very slow tempo, and after several repeats, suddenly jumps into a wildly accelerated finish. In this, the strathspey would seem to have descended from Hungarian tzigane music.

We collect only such strathspeys as have become used

as reels, and which fit into our general category of the sort of square dance music we find exciting to play.

RANTS

Rants are curious old pieces which were designed to be played at the fastest possible tempo — something like double the normal brisk tempo of other square dance music. In fact, the tunes were probably composed for musical competitions, to see who could keep up the fastest pace on fiddle, flute, or pipe.

Some rants are in 6/8 or 9/8 time, others in 2/4. They may have a repetition of phrases which would sound very dull at a normal tempo. But the very great speed and intensity with which they are played gives them a hypnotic, perpetual-motion effect, seemingly without beginning or end. Rants are best played late of an evening, when everybody has had plenty of stimulation. They are wild. They may be an acquired taste, but I love them.

REELS AND HORNPIPES

There is no need to differentiate between reels and hornpipes, so far as the music is concerned. For the past two hundred years at least, the tunes have been interchangable. Some have been printed with titles like *Rose-Bud Reel* or *Mountain Hornpipe*. (An interesting tune, by the way, which I remember hearing the old-timers play when I was small, and I wondered then if I could ever learn the damn thing; with the original grace notes — *four* grace notes together, not just one —

it is about as easy to play as Heifetz's version of *Hora Staccato*.)

For some reason — probably because they are so easy and simple — the reel and hornpipe tunes everyone knows, and which are played to death, are those we would rate the poorest. For example, *Soldier's Joy* or *Sailor's Hornpipe*. What modern composer, writing anything from a comic opera to a TV commercial which pertained to the sea, hasn't dredged up some version of that tired old *Sailor's Hornpipe*?

To choose a melody, for comparative purposes, against which reels and hornpipes may be judged, *Ladies' Walpole Reel* will do well enough. (It was known before 1850 as *Massai's Favorite*.) It hasn't a repeated measure, or even a repeated phrase, through both strains; the last measure of the first strain is not an ending, but a lead into the second strain; and the second strain, contrasting with the first, builds up to a fine climax.

Some good tunes, to be sure, do have repeated measures or repeated phrases. But such repetition must have a melodic reason, and there must be sufficient expression in the playing, such as varying emphasis, to avoid monotony.

We suspect that it is the deadly repetitive character of nearly all square dance music heard in recent years, that has led to its total lack of esteem, and its neglect for such a long time, by educated musicians and music lovers generally. And I certainly don't blame them.

What interests me is how square dance music reached

such a low ebb. And we have decided that the repetitive nature of so much of this music came about for two reasons.

First, over the centuries many melodies were handed down by ear, without notes, and by the time they came to be written down, difficult phrases had been lost, and repeated phrases substituted. Second, many many tunes were composed by people who created them entirely out of bits and pieces of earlier tunes.

Perhaps the best way to sum up our definition of good square dance music is to say that each melody must have some character or quality that sets it apart from all others, and which makes it usually impossible to be imitated successfully.

The appeal of this music to the listener is, of course, almost entirely dependent on the ability of the performer. The composer-conductor, André Previn (lately of the London Symphony) says something to the effect that every performance of classical music can be a new beginning, a chance to improve on any previous performance. The same applies at least as much to good square dance music.

This is not meant to make square dance music sound discouraging to instrumental beginners. Kids love it. And there is plenty of it that can be played, by novice musicians, at least as well as they can play anything else at the same tempo.

Nevertheless, it is axiomatic to say that the faster the pace in any kind of music, the harder it is to attain a high degree of expression and interpretation. Certainly there is not a great amount of classical music, in which note follows note with such a continuous rapidity as in some square dance music.

And so we find that the more talented and able the musician, the more chance square dance music offers for the development and improvement of technique. This is mainly why this music has such a lasting fascination for those of us who play it. A fascination that does not diminish, year after year after year, no matter how many times we may have played some of the tunes.

MISS RAMSAY'S BOOK

A COUPLE OF YEARS AGO a Scottish friend gave me a handsome old book of music, half-bound in leather — about ten by twelve inches, 148 pages. On the outside there are only the words, MISS RAMSAY OF BARNTON, inlaid in gold on a patch of red leather.

Inside the cover there is a signature, probably of Miss Ramsay's mother, "HON*ble* M*rs.* RAMSAY OF BARNTON", and a hand-written index. It would appear that several collections of music put out by Niel Gow & Son's, Edinburgh, had been made into one privately-bound volume for Miss Ramsay.

At first I though the book just a quaint antique. But more careful study revealed it to be an authoritative record of exactly how a great many of our familiar jigs and reels were scored and played in the eighteenth century — the golden age of square-dance music.

No date appears in the book. But on doing a bit of research, I found that the publisher, Niel Gow, a violinist and composer of some note, was born in 1727 and died in 1807. His son and partner, Nathaniel, died in 1831. From these facts and other data, it would seem that the Ramsay book must have been bound between 1803 and 1807. But the first section (a second printing) was the work of Niel Gow, before his son came into the business, and may well have been first issued as early as 1775. Nathaniel Gow's autograph can be seen, in faded ink, on some of the later sections.

The written material — introductions, dedications, and so forth — amply illustrates my theory that "country music" began as highly sophisticated "city music." The Gow firm issued all its collections under the general title of *The Complete Repository,* Part First, Part Second, and so on. Each was elaborately dedicated to some lady of social prominence, often a "Dutchess" (sic), and some of these inscriptions are quite instructive historically.

The first section is called "Part First of the Complete Repository of Original Scots Slow Strathspeys and Dances for the Harp, Piano-forte, Violin, Violoncello, &c. Humbly Dedicated to Her Grace the Dutchess of Gordon," and has the note below, "80 of the Tunes will suit the German Flute and the whole may be adapted for Military Bands."

The elaborate dedication follows:

> The Publishers. . . . would be wanting in the Duty they owe to your Grace, were they not to embrace the Opportunity to Ackknowledge the very great Obligation they lay under to your Grace, and how much it is owing, to

your Grace's kind patronage that so great a preference has hitherto been given to the Setts of Scots Strathspeys and Reels published by Niel Gow & Son's.

In presenting the present to the Public, which is the first time those tunes in the Stile as played by Niel Gow have been in print, it has been the Object of the Publishers to preserve them for the Amateurs of that Stile of Music in their Native Simplicity, and free from the Corruption of Whim or Caprice, and the Publishers humbly hope they will be received by your Grace and their numerous other Friends and the Public at large as a testimony to their profound Gratitude, and Respect, and we have the Honour to be your Grace's much Obliged and Devoted Humble Servants, NIEL GOW & SON'S."

We can see, from the next dedication, that well toward two centuries ago, the Gows could already complain that square-dance music was being desecrated by certain musicians — much as I have complained in earlier chapters here. The Gows' language may be a bit more flowery, but no less emphatic:

To HER GRACE THE DUTCHESS OF BUCCLEUGH, With great deference and respect, we lay this Second Volume of our REPOSITORY before your Grace and the public.

THE ORIGINAL SCOTS STRATHSPEYS, REELS,

AND JIGS, of which this Collection Consists, are brought forward with a view, to serve as a STANDARD of those NATIONAL TUNES AND DANCES: for, we Cannot avoid mentioning, that in every part of SCOTLAND where we have occasionally been, and from every observation we were able to make, have not ONCE met with TWO PROFESSIONAL MUSICIANS who play the SAME notes of ANY tune. This being the Case, the Standard now proposed, will we hope, appear abundantly apparent; and that a CONFORMITY in playing those tunes, may with great propriety be adopted. We are encouraged to entertain this idea, from the favourable reception which our former publications have received from the Public, whose approbation, with that of your GRACE, we shall always esteem, and be proud to acknowledge. In the hope, that our efforts to add to the stock of NATIONAL music, will have a happy attendency, we send this Collection forth into the world; and will deem ourselves gratified to hear, that it meets with approving reception, We have the honour. . . ." etc. etc.

The subject of uniformity is mentioned again in yet another dedication, to the Countess of Loudoun and Moira:

". . . . having succeeded so far by our first two parts as to obtain the approbation of Amateurs, as well as Professional Musicians, WE

70

now venture to submit this our Third part of the Complete Repository, and we humbly trust our Endeavors to conciliate an uniformity in playing these tunes will soon be Established in every part of the Island...."

After the formal fastidiousness of these lines to her Ladyship, it is a bit of a jolt to find the first selection entitled *Drunk at Night and Dry in the Morning.*

For those who may share my own interest in titles, here are a few more from the Ramsay book: *Petty Coat Loose; Bung Your Eye* (Same tune as the one I have scored as *Brisk Young Lads,* the Irish title by which I knew it.) *What the Devil Ails You; My Wife is a Wee Wanton Thing; The Old Man Will Never Die; The Piper's Maggot; Merrily Danced the Quaker's Wife* (probably a tune not popular with the anti-dancing, fanatically un-merry Quakers of that day.) *Rise ye Lazy Lubber; Lick the Ladle Sandy; Kiss Me Fast, My Minnie's Comming; Put the Gown on the Bishop; O', She's Comical; Guzzle Together; The Feet Washing; Rock and a Wee Pickle Tow; Off She Goes* (a lively jig scored exactly, note for note, as we played it when I was small) ; *Col Upton's Conceit* (Nath. Gow was favored with this dance by the Countess of Mansfield — must have been quite a moment for young Nath., as he had it so recorded in print under the score!) ; *The Mole Catcher's Daughter; Largo's Fairy Dance; The Mad (or Poor) Boy.*

Most of us have taken for granted that the cult of fanatics who go about tracking folk themes from among dock-workers, or cowboys, or migrant laborers or hoboes, is a modern development. And that our fashionable troubadors who have popularized this sort of melody in recent years had discovered a new technique.

Actually Nathaniel Gow, who fancied himself as a sort of Cole Porter to the aristocratic smart set of his time, was doing the same thing around 1800. He composed *The Mad (or Poor) Boy* by elaborating on the lines he had heard being chanted by a young beggar. As he puts it, underneath the title — "From the Original as Sung by him in the streets of Edinburgh." And by way of further authentication, there is a short line of scored notes preceding the composition, with the legend, "The Original as sung by the Boy", and below it, "The Boy frequently repeats this Barr, 'Fat Meat's Bonny, Fat Meat's Bonny', while he looks around him expecting Alms, which his truly Simple apperance Seldome fail to insure to him."

Incidentally, the first part of this composition, in 4/4 time and labelled "Very slow, with Expression" strikes me as pretty dull stuff. But then Gow goes on and develops his theme in 9/8 time, and the result is a rather pleasing jig.

Another of Nathaniel Gow's efforts along these lines is entitled *Callar, Herring* and is based on some notes said to be "The Original Cry of the Fish Women". (Burl Ives, or the Seegers, should love this one.) Throughout the score, there are textual notes showing where different strains were inspired — "Coming East along George Street" or "Three different fish Women in St. Andrews Square", etc. and so on.

But for me the happiest discovery was a Gow master-piece called *Largo's Fairy Dance* which was: "Composed (by the Desire) & Dedicated to, the Members of the Fife Hunt". One of the square-dance tunes we used in the old days at home, and have used again recently, was always known as *The Fairy Dance,* but we had no idea of its origin. Here is positive proof that it was written by Nathaniel Gow; probably between 1800 and 1805. It is the second part of his *Largo's Fairy Dance* and follows a rather elaborate slow march. Our version of the tune is for the most part faithful to the original, but we had lost a few nice little touches, somewhere along the line, as the piece was handed down over the past 160 years or so. But I hope that old Nathaniel would agree that at least we have always played his tune "With Spirit", as his own notation directs.

Another typical Gow touch is the notation on some of his more sentimental pieces: "Pathetickly Slow."

I was especially pleased with the Gows' reference to the "German flute". Some of my fiddler friends have seemed to be a little doubtful about my contention that flutes were more sought after than fiddles, during the golden age of square-dance music. Finding this particular mention of the flute further supports the theory.

A flute with metal keys, enabling a full chromatic range of three octaves, was still called the German flute in the early 1800s, because it had not long been known in England. Mozart, who had died in 1791 and was already considered quite generally to be the greatest of all composers, had shown a strong preference for the flute in its then newly improved form.

Until the arrival of the German flute the musicians of the British Isles had, for woodwinds, mostly only such limited and comparatively ineffectual instruments as recorders, six-holed pipes or fifes, and the ancient shawm which was also a holed pipe, with a horn at the end. These were no match in virtuosity with fiddles, of course. The keyed flute from Germany brought a whole new dimension and brilliance to the playing of square-dance music.

Then in the later 1800s, when square-dance music began to fade from the scene in cities and the homes of the rich, flutes began to disappear, and the fiddles again took over. The reason was simple. In the poorest and most remote homes of Scotland and Ireland, and in the New World, violins could be repaired indefinitely, and indeed new ones built, by craftsmen using only simple hand tools. Materials were readily available and cost nothing.

Flutes, on the other hand, were very difficult and expensive to manufacture, requiring precision workshops and specially trained experts. The barrels were of wood (metal was a more recent development) and soon cracked and were not repairable. The metal keys could not be made by hand.

And so, wherever square-dance music survived, it was usually kept alive only by fiddlers. And the prominent part that flutes and other wind instruments had once played, when square-dance music had been the height of fashion, was almost wholly forgotten. The decline in the quality of the tunes, and the manner in which they were played, was inevitable.

I have spent many a happy hour poring over the thick, hand-blocked pages of Miss Ramsay's old book, with its beautifully engraved scores. And as I follow the notes, I try to imagine the sound of Niel Gow's well-balanced orchestra, putting on a spirited and polished performance of jigs and reels, at a fashionable "rout" in Edinburgh or London. Compared to the synthetic rustics we now hear on television, banging away on electric guitars and fiddles, those old musicians must have sounded like a symphony.

As for our own group, we can only make a guess — from circumstantial evidence — as to how closely we can reproduce the sound and style of so long ago. For my part, I like to be guided by the reaction of those who hear us. And when our listeners are genuinely excited by the music itself, and not just because it is a novelty, or because it is "antique", then I feel we must be getting close to the standards of the square-dance ensembles of the old days.

8

Beethoven Discovers
Square Dance Music

Usually people think I am trying to put them on when I mention Beethoven's renditions of our square dance music — even people of much wider acquaintance with the great composer's work than I could claim. You might as well try to tell them that Bach once wrote some swing music. They are hardly convinced even when they hear the recent recording of this very little known Beethoven opus.

In 1817 a successful Edinburgh music publisher, George Thomson, asked several of the best Continental composers to create for him some pieces based on the traditional folk tunes of the British Isles. The publication of such music, he thought, should bring considerable prestige to his firm.

Beethoven didn't reply at the time, though two or three other composers accepted the invitation. But in 1818, perhaps because he had run short of funds, the famous German genius (then about 48) wrote Thomson he would have a try at writing twelve "themes with variations" on payment of a hundred ducats in cash.

Beethoven was fond of English literature, but it would seem he had little or no interest in the music of the British Isles. He referred to the themes he used as Scottish airs, though some were Irish and others old English. Very likely he didn't know the difference, nor could care less, so long as he received those ducats — equal to about $200.

There is no evidence that the appearance of this particular work added any lustre to Beethoven's reputation at home. As for any Scots who may have heard them, the compositions probably sounded as incongruous as they do to me today. When I first heard the recording, I thought it must have been intended as a parody. But so far as I could check the matter out, that kind of humor did not exist for Beethoven. He was merely doing his best, in his careful classical German style, to make a little musical silk purse out of what he must have felt was a pretty hairy sow's ear. The dismal tunes used for his themes, however he came by them, are surely among the worst of their kind.

Why would Beethoven, then the most sophisticated composer yet heard in the western world, choose such commonplace themes? And why would he write them down in a manner that ignores the tempo, rhythm and expression so essential in endowing this kind of music with any appeal at all?

It has been said that he chose the dullest and simplest tunes in order to demonstrate his virtuosity at developing variations. This doesn't seem logical to me. He had no need for such tricks. He was already famous for his magnificently complex and innovative symphonies.

It seems more likely that the German master simply didn't know there were any better folk melodies of Ireland and Scotland, lands he had never visited. So he wrote out his themes so they would sound as much as possible like the German folk tunes he knew; slow, mechanical beat, and precise equal note-values of a Bach fugue for the harpsichord. Only Victor Borge could do proper justice to music such as this — but to do it, the Great Dane would have to know what real square dance music sounds like. And probably, like Beethoven, he still doesn't. What a pity!

By the way, I forgot to mention (for the benefit of our musicologist friends) that the portion of the Beethoven work for Thomson that is of interest here, is entitled *Opus 105, Six Themes and Variations for Flute and Piano.* The fifth and sixth themes are traditional-style Irish jigs in 6/8 time, of the same brisk rhythm as, for example, *Garry Owen.* At least they *were,* until Beethoven got hold of them.

The fifth theme is like the endless hundreds we've played in our researches over the years — even *The Irish Washerwoman* sounds distinguished by comparison.

The sixth is familiar from square dances of my youth, and we knew the notes just as Beethoven scored them, a typical jig called *Paddy Whack.* Not so dull as the fifth, it is still far below top level in spirit and melodic quality, compared to many of our fine Irish jigs that were well known in the British Isles and even in the New World in Beethoven's time.

Ardent lovers of Beethoven may take all this as some sort of insult to one of the great immortals of music. Nothing like that is intended on my part. Actually the *Variations,* after they have left their beginning themes behind, become rather pleasant and interesting compositions. What fascinates me is to speculate on what would have happened, had Thomson provided Beethoven with some of the better themes, such as *The Brisk Young Lads* and *Swimming in the Gutter,* and if Beethoven had ever heard such music played by someone of the calibre of the Gows. Perhaps he would have written something that would have become as lastingly popular, but more distinctive, than Lizst's *Hungarian Rhapsodies* which were based on tzigane folk tunes.

Anyway, we can easily imagine how Beethoven, in those insularized times, may have used the only Irish and Scottish themes he happened to know. It is much harder to figure out why American composers of the twentieth century have been quite happy to remain equally ignorant.

Whenever one of these composers, however sophisticated in all other respects, has occasion to produce a scherzo of Irish folk flavor, we always hear some simpleminded jig like *St. Patrick's Day in the Morning.* Anything pertaining to ships, or the sea, and our ears are treated to yet another bastardization of *Sailor's Hornpipe.* Bucolic or western oriented works are always adorned with bits of *Turkey in the Straw* or *Oh, Susannah.* The last two being played, as often as not, as background music for some portrayal of a historic event that

79

took place long before they were written. (Both were minstrel show tunes, *not* square dance music.)

One of the most venerable and celebrated of modern composers comes up our way now and then. He is also well known as a leading critic and an expert on music generally, old and new. At a party one night, he was conversing with the lady who had recently become our pianist at the Nelson square dances. Somehow he got the idea she was associated with Monadnock Music, a summer classical group, and he started questioning her about the sort of music they played.

She meanwhile took for granted he was referring to our square dance music group, which I'm sure at that time he had never heard of. When she told him we usually played only jigs, reels, and hornpipes, his obvious astonishment tipped her off. She was pretty embarrassed, but the old maestro tried to be helpful. He then told us of a book we would find absolutely indispensable in our researches. It was the Final, Complete Authority on music such as ours, the one and only reference work he had himself relied on for years.

Afterward, at quite some trouble and expense, we managed to get the book. It proved to be the largest collection of worthless and hackneyed junk ever put between two covers, so far as we were concerned. Everything from *The Mockingbird* to *Polly Wolly Doodle*. Not a single decent old jig, reel, or hornpipe was mentioned. Our composer friend must have thought we were trying to start a local branch of Grand Ole Opry.

The joke, however, was not entirely on us, we finally concluded. For in our own researches and efforts at explaining our music, nothing could be more encouraging than to find how little the accepted experts had done in this field.

Oddly enough, in the comparatively modern work of Stravinsky (the idol of all of us who play woodwinds) certain passages have the true flavor of classic eighteenth century square dance music — in contrast to Beethoven's jaded and mechanical Irish themes. Stravinsky's *Pulcinella Suite,* written originally for a ballet produced in 1919, includes a lively tarantella which could pass for a traditional old Irish jig, so far as the score and the tempo are concerned. (The tarantella being an ancestor of the Irish jig.) If played with the typical Irish lilt — a hint of syncopation that can't be indicated by notation, incidentally — the resemblance would be complete.

In *Pulcinella* Stravinsky took themes from Pergolesi, the versatile Italian composer who died in 1736. And so we find Stravinsky writing what sounds like a fine Irish jig of ancient character. He found it perfectly suited to a particular movement of his ballet; and the piece has since become a popular symphony concert number. But today few listeners, probably, or even the musicians playing it, are aware of its real origin and character — since it is no very close relative of *The Irish Washerwoman.*

Who knows, maybe we'll live to see a day when some competent modern composer will use some of the best of the authentic old themes we've revived. It would take a bit of doing. First of all, as we've tried to indicate elsewhere, they are not easy. As a long-time first flute player in one of our greatest symphony orchestras remarked the other day, after sampling our *Nelson Music Collection* — his first introduction to square dance music — "You know, these things are goddam hard to play well!" And second, modern compositions of the sort that get rewarded by grants and acclaim from critics these days, are not exactly what many people could think of as wildly gay.

So we may have to wait until "happy music" is again in style, if our music is to be rediscovered by the classical "elite." But we won't lose any sleep over it.

Sweet Potatoes, Brakedrums, Eardrums, and Canticles

One never knows when or from what source inspiration may strike. At least I never do. The following erudite essay was born in large part because my wife had decided to make some pumpkin pies.

Our old friends Jim and Betty Lape were having dinner guests down the road at their weekend retreat. Janet had offered them one of her new-baked pies, and when they came up to get it, they told me about a symphony concert they had heard in Boston. This led to a discussion of certain modern compositions, and I had the feeling my views were not entirely accepted.

Next week the pie plate was left in our mailbox, accompanied by a newspaper clipping (referred to in this piece) with the heading: "Harrison's Canticle No. 3 Proves Fine, Sometimes Surprising."

I hope that my piece resulting from these events didn't cause the serious music-lover readers of the *Berkshire Eagle,* where it recently appeared, too much pain:

If I wanted to start feeling old, I would reflect that people my age can remember when composers we now regard as traditional and conservative, were knocked by the critics as wild, iconoclastic, crude, vulgar. Such accolades were bestowed on Ravel, Stravinsky, Sibelius, Copland, and others. Yet none of these composers, so far as I know, ever wrote music featuring the jew's harp, washtubs, or kazoo.

Musical people tell me the present *Boston Globe* critic, Michael Steinberg, is rough on traditional music, and soft on the modern stuff. It's even been said that some performers would not return to Boston, they'd been so disgruntled by Steinberg's acid comments.

I'm inclined to take such gossip with a grain of salt. But somebody just sent me a clip of Steinberg's review of Lou Harrison's ultra-modern composition called *Canticle No. 3,* and it does seem to be a bit slanted.

I had happened to hear the Boston Symphony performance, via TV. The piece is scored for only two melody instruments, ocarina and guitar, all the rest being various drums and bells, several lengths of iron water pipe, and eight old brakedrums. The latter I couldn't see well enough to identify, but the loudest pair sounded to me as though they had come from the front wheels of a 1955 Plymouth.

This I thought very unfortunate, and I'm appalled to find that a critic's ear could be so calloused as not to feel such a lack of tonal quality. I used to play the brakedrums a bit myself, and took a few lessons from the head mechanic down at Fairfield's garage one winter. He was a real virtuoso, and seldom touched anything but 1930

Cadillac drums. He could handle a pair of seven-eighths ring-wrenches like Gene Krupa.

But he also conceded that my own drums — Packard 1926, 21-inch wheels — had a pretty mellow tone, probably because they'd been grooved up from so much running in deep mud. In later years, for some special occasion like a square dance in the town hall, I would sometimes remove the rear drums from my old Silver Ghost Rolls Royce. The only trouble was, they were in the key of E-flat, and I had to transpose everything.

Well, anyway, Mr. Steinberg came out strong for *Canticle No. 3,* quoting composer-critic Virgil Thomson, who once called it "lovely to listen to." I hate to disagree with Virgil, but the sounds that reached my ears reminded me of somebody blowing on a beer bottle in Cousin Harvey's welding shop while Harv was pounding on a set of andirons.

Maybe I'm biased because of the title. Cute or arch titles always tend to turn me off. Technically, a canticle must have real singing in it, and there's no singing at all in this thing. Also, a canticle is supposed to relate to biblical texts, and the chariots of biblical times did not have brakedrums — just straps around the horses' rumps (we used to call them "hold-backs") and of course you couldn't very well play a tune on them. Though sometimes the horses themselves — well, never mind.

This so-called canticle does have some pretty nice silences in it, as mentioned by Steinberg. In modern music, a silence is comparable to modern paintings with blank canvasses or empty frames. For my part, these silences were the best passages, only they didn't last long enough. Furthermore, I couldn't tell just what key some of the silences were played in, which was confusing.

I was disappointed that the Boston Symphony hadn't used Model-T Ford foot-brake drums for the silences. This would have rounded out the effect, as the foot-brake of the Model-T had no drums. It had only a wheel in the transmission with a contracting band around it; when it didn't work, you stepped on the reverse pedal for quick stops.

But maybe I shouldn't be too hard on Steinberg, as he's obviously still pretty young. He refers to "exotic instrumentation" and says that when this canticle was written, in the early 1940s, such sounds "would have been totally unfamiliar to just about everyone in an American audience."

Evidently he isn't familiar with *The Anvil Chorus, The Whistler and his Dog,* and that Victorian symphony where they shoot off the cannon, and many other classics of my youth — mostly far more mellifluous and gutsy than this sweet potato and brakedrum stuff.

The Anvil Chorus was one of the most popular selections of our family band at the farm when I was small. (I was already pretty good on the ocarina, by the way — a Sears Roebuck key-of-C, thirty five cents plus postage.) Earl Nims, our hired hand and local strong-man, would go out to the barn and get the hundred pound anvil, lug it into the livingroom and pretend to drop it in some girl's lap. When we launched into the classic melody, Earl would pound out the anvil part with a heavy sledge hammer. Afterward, just to show off, he would raise the anvil aloft with one hand. (I wonder if anybody in the Boston Symphony today could do it with both hands.)

It wasn't explained why the ocarina in the *Canticle No. 3* rendition was played by a cellist. As an old hand with this tricky instrument, my guess is that none of the regular woodwind players wanted to be stuck with it. Whereas a string player wouldn't be expected to do anything very amazing with a contraption that blows and has finger-holes, like a very pregnant recorder.

The television announcer informed us that the ocarina is a small wooden instrument. Actually the whole point of the ocarina is that it is made of baked terra cotta. Better known in my youth as the sweet potato, it came in assorted sizes, and was a darn poor substitute for a modern flute, though its weak tone is soft and pleasant.

Of course, when you're discussing the Boston Symphony, it sounds better to say ocarina than sweet potato. (In Italian, ocarina means "little goose" — it's shaped like one, and also sounds like one. I don't know the Italian word for brakedrum, but probably that would sound better too.)

The fact is, electronic devices excepted, none of these so-called exotic instruments is anything new. As a lifetime semi-pro bush-league folk music performer (with a little Mozart on the side) I've heard all kinds; musical glasses, shotgun barrels played like a bugle, you name it. Once I made a pretty majestic sounding alpenhorn out of a plastic drainpipe. Recently, I began rehearsing again *The Stars and Stripes Forever,* including the piccolo obbligato, playing it on a dandelion stem.

When it comes to truly subtle orchestrations, I submit that Spike Jones and his band, some thirty years ago, reached a preeminence that will long endure unrivalled in musical history. They used everything from musical saws and klaxon horns to motorbike engines and firecrackers. I still have the classic Jones recording of a Hawaiian medley. It ends with Spike intoning, in *true* canticle style, to the strains of *Aloha Oe,* "And now we must bid goodbye to those enchanted isles, as our ship sinks slowly in the west . . ."

Note: Musicians who wish to take up the brakedrums should lose no time in obtaining them. For a whole set of eight, at least two old cars are needed. Most new cars are already coming through with disk brakes, and old abandoned cars everywhere are being hauled away by the environmentalists.

Collecting, Composing, and Decomposing

It's going to be kind of hard to end this little book, because more things keep happening. Like, last week we were joined by a real, live oboe player — from New York or somewhere. Have you ever known an oboe player? It used to be said they all eventually went nuts, something about pressure on the ears leaking into the brain. I think the rumor began just because they look so funny. To hold onto that little double reed, resembling a pinched dandelion stem, an oboe player must have no lips at all, or suck them in so he looks as though he hadn't any; and whenever he blows, his mouth is twisted up in a maniacal grin. After a few years his face is apt to stay that way all the time.

Our guest oboeist was pretty good, and soon began to get onto the rhythms of our idiom. Probably because he was still quite young, he didn't act very much crazier than some of our other musicians. But we did some more or less wild improvised woodwind duets, and the banshee shrieks of the oboe startled some of the dancers so much they forgot what they were supposed to be doing.

There were about two hundred people up at the village hall that evening, and it was interesting to note the reaction to the sound of a single oboe added to the fourteen or so other instruments in the group. Most people cheered and clapped. But a few of the young married set — these are always the most conservative in their tastes — were somewhat upset by this unfamiliar sound. One chap even shouted up at me, "You ought to send that goddamn long haired whistler right back to whereever he came from!"

I tried to appease them, at intermission, by explaining that the oboe had been a traditional instrument in square dance music, in Europe, for centuries. (It used to be called the hautboy — pronounced oh boy, not hot boy.)

Another recent happening that kept us busier than usual was the publication of our *Nelson Music Collection*. This contains 60 melodies, each one selected because it seemed to us an archetype of its kind. And at the end, just for fun, we added three tunes of my own invention. At least I think they're my own, but maybe they came from an atavistic memory of things that were played by some of my ancestors in Scotland or somewhere.

About the last thing that would have crossed my mind was the idea of publishing a book of music. It began with a notebook of things for our own use, mostly transcribed by Kay Gilbert, whose mind is more methodical than my own. We had found ourselves lugging around a stack of bulky books, many old and falling apart, and some containing only two or three pieces we would ever use.

The notebook was a great convenience. But as we played here and there, more and more people began to ask for copies of it. And finally the only practical solution we could figure out was to get our collection published.

We might have thought twice about it if we had foreseen the technical problems and the time (more than a year) it would take to solve them. Square dance music that is printed in the modern standard manner, in a reasonable page-size, is unattractive and hard to read. Kay finally solved that problem by merely designing staffs of special spacing and dimensions, and spending a few thousand hours hand-drawing all the scores. Of course this effort was helped some by the discovery that she possessed a most unusual natural talent for handling drawing tools.

Then it took us months to learn that people in the music business have at least one thing in common with people in most other businesses. Always on the lookout for something "unusual or different," when shown something that actually is different, they at once want to know what category they can fit it into. Like "country music," maybe? What do we compare it with?

Well, of course we could only say that if there *were* anything at all similar to our collection, we wouldn't have had to beat our brains out putting the thing together; and there would have been little demand for it. But this was apparently not an acceptable answer. After awhile I began to feel as if I were trying to sell phony stock certificates or something.

Within a couple of weeks after we finally got the collection printed, we were already more than satisfied that it had all been well worth the effort. After all, there is nothing more satisfying than genuine appreciation from people whose judgement you can respect. Even if the book ultimately turns out to bring in little more money than we put into it, we'll still be happy — it wasn't done with any great expectation of fame or fortune.

We are sometimes asked why we printed only melodies, without accompaniments. There are other reasons, aside from the additional work and greatly enlarged space needed. For centuries, the piano, or other accompanying instruments, were played mostly by ear. A musician with a good natural ear can soon learn how to improvise proper chords for each melody. A really good accompanist, however, must have a knack for this idom, as well as experience.

As for the other instruments, playing harmony or obbligatoes, we sometimes write out the parts. But generally this is done by ear, improvising. Monotony is avoided, when playing a melody over and over several times, by inventing a different second part each time through, and by different instruments alternating in taking a lead part.

I remember one old fellow, just moved into town from upcountry somewhere, who offered to play the piano for us at a dance. When we asked him what music he knew, he said, "Oh, it don't make no difference, I can play chords for anything!" And it turned out that he could. Two chords in G major. He banged them out all evening, regardless of what tune we might be playing or whatever the key.

We can only wonder, at this point, what the future of square dance music will be. It has been around about as long as any music that is played today, but there have been those periods when the best of it, and the classic techniques of playing it, have been almost forgotten.

Have we reached a peak in reviving the old music, or have we only made a start? The latter, I hope. Anyway, I would like to do a lot more with it in whatever few years I may still be able to play. And I have an almost mystical faith in all the younger people, and the kids — some of them now starting to make music a career — because these are the people whose enthusiasm has kept us working at it.

It has now become possible, as this goes to press, to mention one further event on our music front — *ebollimento accelerando!* Our own recording, pieced together from a few hundred miles of tapes, has finally burst forth to startle the eardrums of music lovers everywhere. It's still too soon for me to be objective about it; so far, my wife has only played it five or six times a day for about three months. But I can say this: if you want to get the ultimate kick that comes only from making a first disk, wait until you're past sixty before you start working on it.

About five years ago, Jim Spaulding, a friend who had made a hobby of taping square dance music, offered to

work with us on any weekends that we could get together. Our first tape sounded discouragingly bad to
us. So the second year we started getting new top-quality
instruments. Kay Gilbert began with a new grand piano,
and I with a new Haynes silver C flute. Later we added
a Haynes alto flute (they make only eight a year, and
it took us three years to get delivery) and a Haynes
piccolo. As there was no chance of our finding other
musicians who knew the music well enough and had
unlimited time to spend, Kay and I decided to make a
recording using only flute and piano.

Meanwhile, we had published *The Nelson Music
Collection,* and decided to tape its entire contents. After
a couple of years of hard work, with many taping ses-
sions, this was finally finished. Then another friend,
Cal Howard, who works for the recording company,
edited the tape. It required cutting out about two-
thirds of the material, ending up with exactly enough
for one forty-five minute LP record. Cal managed it
with fanatical dedication; he is the only professional
in the business, I'm sure, who happens to know our
music well.

I had thought the first pressing would last a year, if
not forever. It was sold out in less than three months,
before we had even got started on any advertising or
much distribution. So now we have a second and much
larger pressing just appearing, hot off the griddle.

Aside from the nature of the music, and the shortcomings of some of my playing (I have since had a
major operation on two faulty fingers, which turned
out a complete success), the record is of some technical

interest to the flute-playing community. It seems that in the process of recording our old melodies, quite by chance, we have produced what is probably the only record employing two C flutes, an alto flute, and a piccolo, played by the same person with various harmonic combinations. This we did at the suggestion of Jim Spaulding, who showed me how to become twins — using dual taping.

Yesterday morning I got a long-distance call from a very pleasant elderly lady who lives alone except for an elderly German Shepherd named Fritz. She had got our record about a month ago and just wanted to tell me how much she enjoyed it. She puts it on every morning before breakfast, she said, and it puts her in a good mood for the rest of the day. After she had gone on in this vein for some time, I asked her, "How does Fritz like it?" and she said, "Oh, he doesn't seem to mind it at all!"

I wouldn't trade a phone-call like that for a ten-thousand dollar grant from the National Endowment for the Arts, or whatever it is they call that thing.

A Few Selected Titles

THE TITLES presented here are only a small part of our total repertoire. The idea is to show a representative selection of melodies of all types (that we consider worthwhile) which were played before the decline of square dance music early in this century. This may help those who would like to learn how to identify and collect, for themselves, melodies of some special interest.

Titles like *Cincinnati* and *Pacific Slope* suggest compositions of fairly late origin. Many others we know to be well over two centuries old. Some of the older titles may not be the original ones; we've simply taken them from the oldest or most authentic scores we happened to find.

Occasionally some tune will be called a reel in one collection, and a hornpipe in another. One learns, with some practice, to identify many versions of the same basic melody, which have become known at different times and places under a number of titles. We try to select the most interesting version, in musical terms;

perhaps not always the most authentic, in terms of actual age. We also try to eliminate the thousands of purely imitative tunes, which make up a large part of so many collections both old and new.

REELS

Chorus Jig

Cicilian Circle

Inimitable

Irish-American

Kiss Me, Joe

Ladies' Walpole

Lardner's

Levantine's Barrel

Miller's

Miss McDonald's

Ned Kendall's Reel

Ostinelli's

Pacific Slope

Peter Street

Pigeon on the Gate

Pig Town Fling

Reed's Favorite

Rose-Bud

Ross's No. 1

Ross's No. 2

Ross's No. 3

Ross's No. 4

St. Agathe

Steamboat Quickstep

Teetotaler's

Wake Up Susan

JIGS

Brisk Young Lads

The Broken Lantern

The Double Head

Garry Owen

Humours of Glen

Maggie Brown's Favorite

Old Dutch Churn

Smash the Window

Swallow Tail

Swimming in the Gutter

American Rifle Team	Ned Kendall's Hornpipe
Atlanta	Old French
Best Shot	President Garfield's
Cincinnati	Quindaro
Democratic	Randall's
Deerfoot	Red Lion
Durang's	Staten Island
Fisher's	Ulster
Forester's	Village Bells
Fred Wilson's	Vinton's
Minneapolis	Wade Hampton's
Miss Mountan's	Youghal Harbor

For purposes of clarification and comparison, there should perhaps be added here another brief list of titles. Those most often heard in recent years, since square dancing was revived. (Tunes I would be happy never to have to play or to hear again.) Some of these may be beloved of callers and dancers. So far as listening is concerned, I think these tunes have caused a nationwide misconception of the potential of truly good square dance music.

These tunes sound just *enough* like the better ones to mislead people into thinking they are hearing the real article. Novice musicians, of course, we would expect to begin with just such simple tunes; just as a novice playing jazz might begin with *Whispering* or *St. Louis Blues* before attempting anything as difficult as Duke Ellington's more sophisticated compositions.

The Arkansas Traveler	Miss McLeod's
Devil's Dream	Money Musk
Hull's Victory	Oh, Susannah
Irish Washerwoman	Rakes of Mallow
Lamplighter's	Soldier's Joy
Little Brown Jug	Turkey in the Straw

MUSIC SCORES

Jig

RAKES OF CLONMEL

BRISK YOUNG LADS

BATCHELDER'S

Reel

SPIRVIN'S FANCY

Reel

HORNPIPE THEME No. 3
by Newton F. Tolman

THE HARE'S FOOT
Rant

Strathspey